The Wild West

Written by Paul Mason
Illustrated by John Gordon

The Wild West: The American Frontier

Two hundred years ago, the western part of the country we now call the United States (US) was called the Wild West. It was a wild land far away from any cities.

Over time, many people began to travel to the Wild West to build their homes and settle there. The country started to grow.

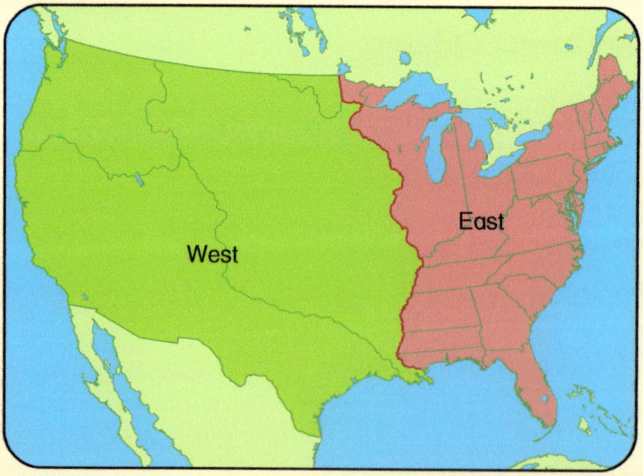

The Wild West was also called the American Frontier. The frontier was as far west as people lived. Beyond that was wilderness.

Life in the Wild West

Life in the Wild West was difficult and travelling there was not easy. There were many dangers for the settlers.

Many different people travelled to the west hoping for a better life. Some were farmers looking for land, some wanted gold and others were looking for adventure.

Let's look at some of the people, places and things from that time.

Native Americans

Native Americans were the first people to live in North America. They lived there long before Europeans came to North America in 1492. The Native Americans were hunters and farmers.

A family of the Blackfoot tribe

There were many different groups of Native Americans – called tribes. Some of the famous tribes were Apache, Cherokee, Blackfoot, Navajo and Sioux. Many of these tribes still exist today.

Sitting Bull

Sitting Bull was a famous chief of the Sioux tribe and a brave and strong leader of his people.

To help the settlers move west, the US government wanted land. Sometimes there were battles between the US army and the Native American tribes over land.

Sitting Bull often led his warriors into battle against the US army. At the famous battle of Little Big Horn, Sitting Bull's warriors defeated General Custer and his army. But the Native Americans couldn't stop the US government taking their land.

The Oregon Trail

The Oregon Trail was one of the paths people took to go west. These paths were sometimes called wagon trails because of the wagons that the settlers travelled in.

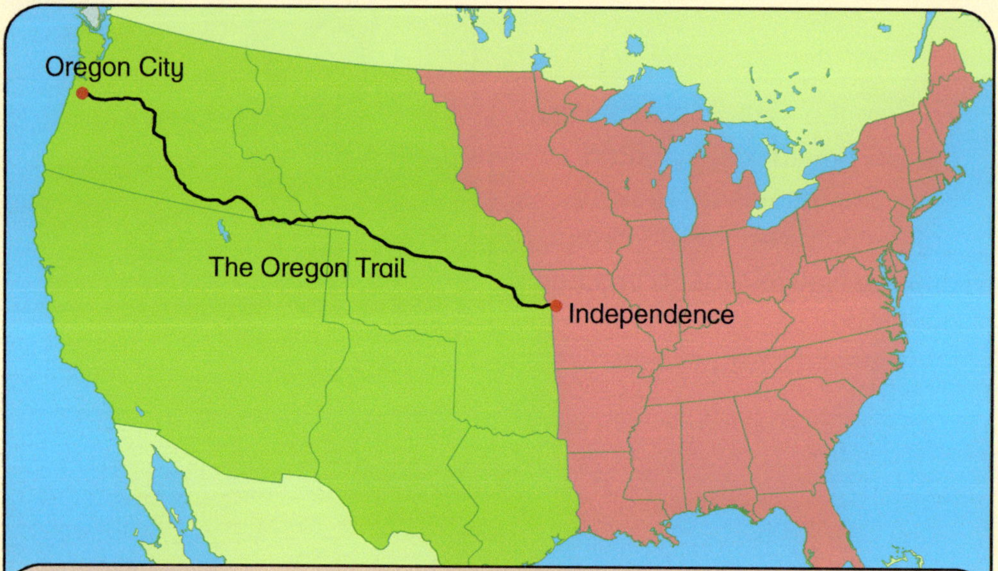

The Oregon Trail was over 3,000 kilometres long!

Thousands of settlers used the Oregon Trail. But not everyone who used the trail got to the end because it was very dangerous. The dangers included disease, snakes, cold weather and wagon accidents.

Daniel Boone and Calamity Jane

Groups of settlers travelling west usually had a leader to show them the way. These leaders were known as frontiersmen.

Probably the most famous frontiersman was Daniel Boone. He was an explorer who found new trails to the west.

Calamity Jane was a famous frontierswoman. She was famous for being a fierce fighter, but also for being very kind to people who needed help.

Hunters and trappers

Some of the first people to travel into the Wild West were hunters and trappers. They went into the wilderness to hunt and trap animals like beavers.

The trappers sold the animal furs, which were used to make clothes. Many furs were sent to Europe on ships.

Later, many hunters went to hunt bison (often called buffalo).

The Gold Rush

Gold was discovered in California in 1848. The news quickly went across the US. Thousands of people travelled west to California. They wanted to get rich. This was called the Gold Rush.

Some people came by ship, while others used the trails over the land.

Towns and cities got bigger and bigger. In the Gold Rush, San Francisco grew from a tiny town into a large city.

Law and order

With more people living in the Wild West, crime became a problem. There were many criminals – called outlaws – as well as lawmen whose job was to stop crime.

A well-known outlaw from this time was Billy the Kid. He was called 'the Kid' because he was so young. Billy the Kid stole horses and cows, as well as robbing and shooting people.

Billy the Kid was finally stopped by sheriff Pat Garett – a famous lawman. Billy was only 21 when he died.

Jesse James

The brothers Jesse and Frank James were two famous Wild West outlaws. They robbed banks and coaches as well as trains. Their gang was known for being very dangerous.

Wyatt Earp was the deputy sheriff of a town called Tombstone. He fought against a gang of outlaw cowboys in a famous gunfight, called the 'Gunfight at the O.K. Corral'.

Cowboys

The grassy plains of the Wild West were also good places to farm cows. The men who looked after the cows were called cowboys. It was a very hard job.

The cowboys had to ride horses and herd lots of cows. They herded them for long distances to sell at the market.

They had to watch the cows all day and all night. They had to sleep and live in the wild. Sometimes they had to fight outlaws who wanted to steal the cows.

Buffalo Bill and Annie Oakley

Buffalo Bill was a cowboy and a buffalo hunter. Later in his life, Buffalo Bill put on big shows which told people all about life as a cowboy in the Wild West. These shows were also called rodeos.

Annie Oakley

Sitting Bull with Buffalo Bill

In Buffalo Bill's Wild West show there was a woman called Annie Oakley. Annie performed tricks with her gun. She could shoot at small targets while riding a horse and people say she never missed a single shot!

Sometimes in the show there were famous guests like Calamity Jane and Sitting Bull!

Tales of the Wild West

Shows like Buffalo Bill's Wild West were very popular. People all around the world wanted to hear stories about the Wild West. There were also books and magazines that told tales about the famous cowboys, lawmen and outlaws.

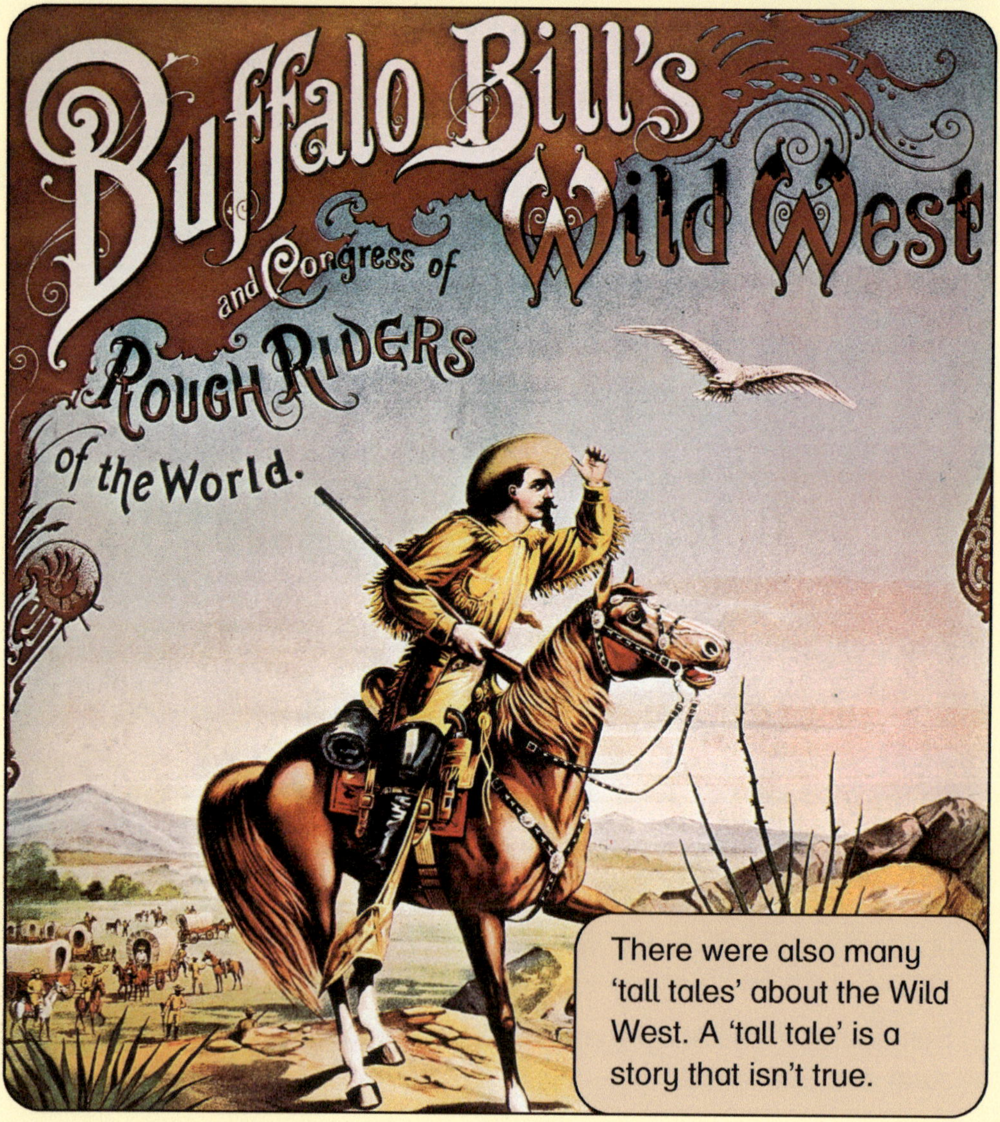

There were also many 'tall tales' about the Wild West. A 'tall tale' is a story that isn't true.

The Tall Tale of Rex Rodeo

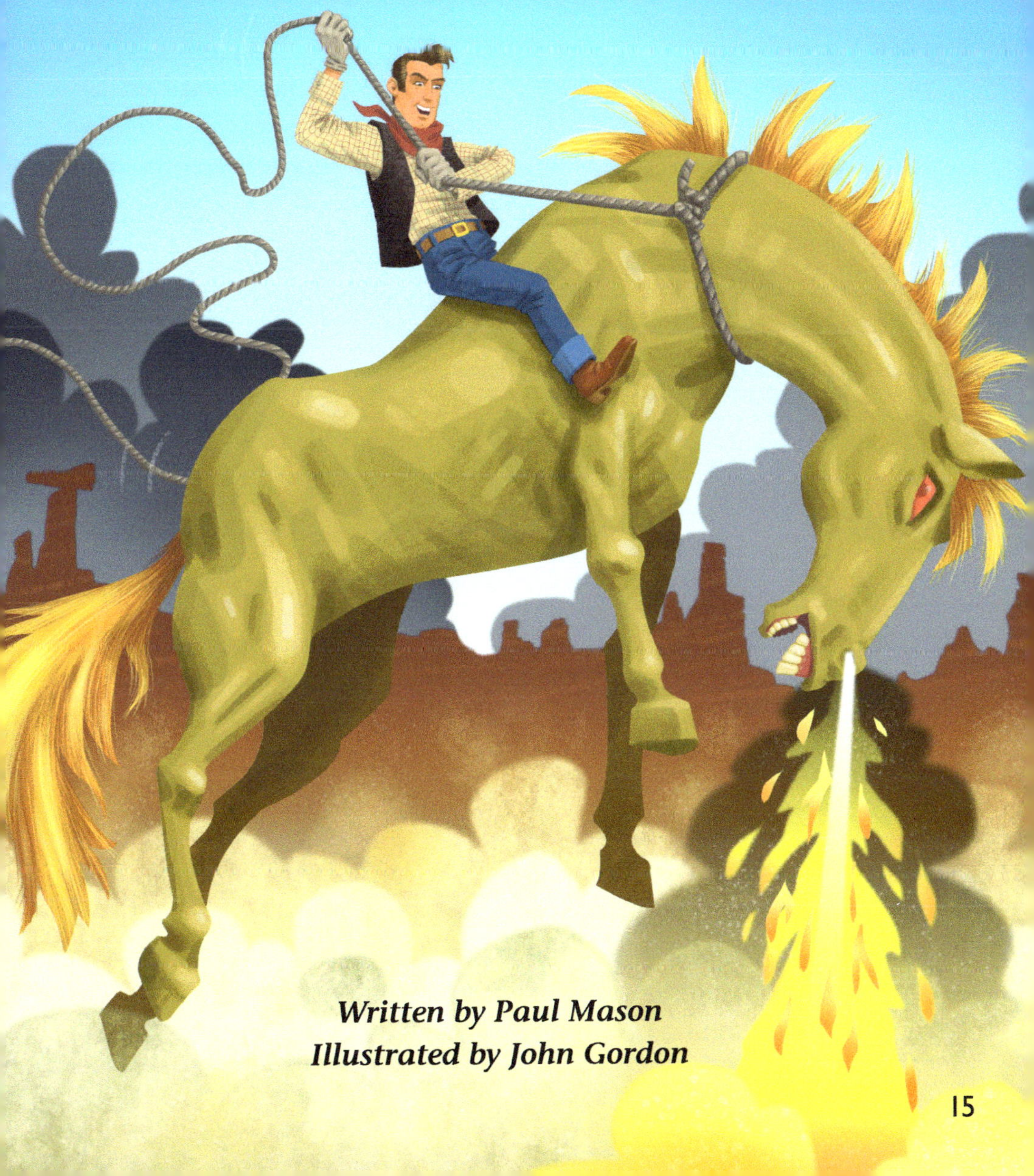

Written by Paul Mason
Illustrated by John Gordon

A long time ago, out on the grassy plains of the Wild West, there lived a brave cowboy called Rex Rodeo. Rex was the biggest, strongest and kindest cowboy in the whole town of Lucky River.
Let me help you with these cows, Mrs Green.
Thank you, Rex.
Rex rode his horse faster than the wind. He caught wild buffalo with his rope. He herded one thousand cows by himself and he helped everyone in the town.

Cowboy Rex was in love with Annie, the mayor's daughter. Annie was beautiful and intelligent, and Rex wanted to marry her.
We will have to ask my father.
I hope he says 'yes'.

But Annie's father, Mayor Milton, was a mean and greedy man who only loved gold.
We want to get married, father.
Are you rich, Rex?
No, I'm poor.

Unlucky for you. If you don't have any money, you can't marry my daughter.
Rex and Annie were very disappointed. What could they do?
I know a way you can marry my daughter.
How?
Tell us, father.
Mayor Milton thought of a plan. The plan was very dangerous, and Mayor Milton knew that Rex might not come back.

Mayor Milton told Rex his plan. Across the river there was a giant horse called Thunder. Thunder was as tall as a tree, with breath of fire, and his tail was made from pure gold.
I want you to catch Thunder and bring him to me! I want his gold tail.
I will catch him!
No! It's too dangerous. You will be killed.
The mayor told Rex that if he brought him Thunder's golden tail, then he could marry Annie.

Brave Rex wasn't worried. He packed some food, some water and his sleeping bag. He said goodbye to Annie.

Rex hopped onto his horse and rode across the shallow river. He rode like the wind out west to the grassy plains, a long way from town.

Then Rex saw Thunder far away. The giant horse made the ground shake with his hooves. Fire roared out of his nostrils and his teeth were like knives.
It's OK, girl!

But Rex wasn't scared. He hid behind a rock and watched quietly. He started to swing his rope around and around.

At the right moment, Rex let go of his rope. The rope flew through the air and landed around Thunder's huge neck.

With a shout, Rex jumped on Thunder's back and held on.

Thunder kicked and danced and made the ground shake, trying to make Rex fall off. The giant horse did not like having Rex on his back. Rex held on for his life!
I'm not letting go!
At last, Thunder lost all his strength and was exhausted. Rex had won!

Rex Rodeo, the bravest cowboy in the West, tied his own horse to Thunder and rode him back to Lucky River.

Back in town, the mayor couldn't believe his eyes. Rex caught Thunder!

Rex gave the mayor the rope to hold the mighty Thunder. But the mayor was frightened of the wild horse.
Here you are, Mayor. You wanted him, now you can have him!
Help!

Suddenly, Thunder let out a big roar of fire. The fire burnt the mayor's shoes, turning them black.

The mayor ran away as fast as he could, with Thunder chasing him, still breathing fire. Mayor Milton was never seen again. The townspeople gathered around Rex.

After that, all was well in Lucky River, out in the grassy plains of the wild, Wild West.

Activities

1 Read and match.

1 Many different people travelled to the west

2 In the Gold Rush, San Francisco grew

3 Daniel Boone was an explorer

4 The Wild West was also called

5 Sitting Bull was a famous chief of the Sioux tribe

6 The trappers sold the animal furs,

a who found new trails to the west.

b from a tiny town into a large city.

c which were used to make clothes.

d and a brave and strong leader of his people.

e hoping for a better life.

f the American Frontier.

2 Who said what? Match the speech bubbles to the pictures.

1 I want you to catch Thunder and bring him to me!

2 I will be home soon. Then we can get married.

3 Rex, you're safe!

4 Look at the golden tail!

5 It's OK, girl!

Mayor Milton

Rex

Annie

3 Find eight hidden words.

v	s	n	t	u	p	o	o	r	s
u	r	l	y	c	k	i	r	l	c
b	l	i	a	g	f	o	c	n	o
s	m	o	v	t	l	i	t	d	w
f	a	j	i	e	l	d	r	h	b
m	y	h	g	e	r	o	d	e	o
g	o	l	d	w	o	l	b	t	y
s	r	u	b	p	n	e	g	r	m
e	g	u	r	l	t	c	k	e	r
f	a	l	u	c	k	y	t	o	l

4 Circle *T* (True) or *F* (False).

1 Sitting Frog was a famous Native American chief. **T** **F**

2 The Oregon Trail was over 3,000 kilometres long. **T** **F**

3 Jesse and Frank James were famous singers. **T** **F**

4 The leaders of wagon trains were called frontiersmen. **T** **F**

5 Gold was discovered in California in 1848. **T** **F**

5 Read and match.

1 A famous sheriff who fought at the Gunfight at the O.K. Corral.

2 A brave and strong leader of the Sioux tribe.

3 A frontierswoman who was a fierce fighter.

4 A famous buffalo hunter who had a Wild West show.

5 A gun shooter who never missed!

6 An outlaw who was very young.

a Buffalo Bill

b Sitting Bull

c Annie Oakley

d Billy the Kid

e Wyatt Earp

f Calamity Jane

6 Put the letters in the correct order.

1 rfreinto frontier

2 terhun ____________

3 sebirt ____________

4 tlria ____________

5 eshor ____________

6 lawuot ____________

7 Read and complete.

cows night cowboys outlaws horses market ~~West~~

Cowboys

The grassy plains of the Wild (1) ___West___ were also good places to farm (2) __________ . The men who looked after the cows were called (3) __________ . It was a very hard job.

The cowboys had to ride (4) __________ and herd lots of cows.
They herded them for long distances to sell at the (5) __________ .
They had to watch the cows all day and all (6) __________ .
They had to sleep and live in the wild. Sometimes they had to fight (7) __________ who wanted to steal the cows.

8 Put the sentences in the correct order.

- [ ] The mayor ran away as fast as he could, with Thunder chasing him, still breathing fire.
- [ ] Rex hid behind a rock and watched quietly.
- [ ] Rex rode like the wind out west to the grassy plains, a long way from town.
- [1] The mayor told Rex that if he brought him Thunder's golden tail, then he could marry Annie.
- [ ] The mayor couldn't believe his eyes. Rex caught Thunder!
- [ ] Rex jumped on Thunder's back and held on.

Bilingual Dictionary

Write the words in your language.

Key: (n) = noun (v) = verb (adj) = adjective

army (n) ____________________
battle (n) ____________________
beaver (n) ____________________
brave (adj) ____________________
breath (n) ____________________
buffalo (n) ____________________
chief (n) ____________________
city (n) ____________________
country (n) ____________________
cowboy (n) ____________________
crime (n) ____________________
dangerous (adj) ____________________
defeat (v) ____________________
disappointed (adj) ____________________
exhausted (adj) ____________________
explorer (n) ____________________
fight (v) ____________________
first (adj) ____________________
frontier (n) ____________________
fur (n) ____________________
gang (n) ____________________
gold (n) ____________________
greedy (adj) ____________________
help (v) ____________________
herd (v) ____________________
home (n) ____________________
hoof (n) ____________________
hop (v) ____________________
hunter (n) ____________________
land (n) ____________________
lawman (n) ____________________
leader (n) ____________________
marry (v) ____________________
mayor (n) ____________________
mean (adj) ____________________
nostril (n) ____________________
outlaw (n) ____________________
pack (v) ____________________
plain (n) ____________________
ride (v) ____________________
roar (v) ____________________
rob (v) ____________________
rodeo (n) ____________________
rope (n) ____________________
settler (n) ____________________
shallow (adj) ____________________
sheriff (n) ____________________
shoot (v) ____________________
sleep (v) ____________________
snake (n) ____________________
steal (v) ____________________
strong (adj) ____________________
target (n) ____________________
trail (n) ____________________
trapper (n) ____________________
tribe (n) ____________________
wagon (n) ____________________
warrior (n) ____________________
wild (adj) ____________________
wilderness (n) ____________________

Macmillan Education
4 Crinan Street
London N1 9XW
A division of Springer Nature Limited

Companies and representatives throughout the world

ISBN 978-1-3800-4194-4

Written by Paul Mason

First published 2015
This edition published 2019

Designed by Carolyn Gibson
Illustrated by John Gordon pp15–27 and Peter Harper pp2, 6
Cover photograph by Getty Images/WorldWideImages
Picture research by Emily Taylor

The authors and publishers would like to thank the following for permission to reproduce their photographs: Alamy Stock Photo/ p4, **Alamy**/The Art Gallery Collection p5(b), Alamy/Everett Collection Historical p10(bl), Alamy/Ewing Galloway p3(tl), Alamy/GL Archive pp8(tl), 10(tr), 11(tl), Alamy/North Wind Picture Archives pp7(tr), 8(b), Alamy/Pictorial Press Ltd p6(bl); **Alamy Stock Photo**/BrownWCannonIII p12(tl); **Corbis** p9(bl), Corbis/Bettmann pp9(tm), 13(tl, tr), 14, Corbis/Julio Donoso/Sygma p12(b), Corbis/HR Locke p7(bl), Photo by Kean Collection/Archive Photos/Getty Images) p3(b); **Getty Images**/Digital Vision Vectors/Grafissimo p5(t), Getty Images/Print Collector/Hulton Archive p11(tr), Getty Images/Westend61 p2.

Printed and bound in Brazil

2025
13